COUNTRIES OF THE WORLD

EGYPT

JOHN PALLISTER

Evans

TITLES IN THE COUNTRIES OF THE WORLD SERIES:
AUSTRALIA • BRAZIL • CHINA • EGYPT • FRANCE • GERMANY ITALY • JAPAN • KENYA • MEXICO • UNITED KINGDOM • USA

Published by Evans Brothers Limited
2A Portman Mansions
Chiltern Street
London W1U 6NR

First published 2004
© copyright Evans Brothers 2004

VISIT OUR WEBSITE
www.evansbooks.co.uk
Evans

British Library Cataloguing in Publication Data
Pallister, John
Egypt. – (Countries of the world)
1.Egypt – Juvenile literature
I. Title
962

ISBN 0 237 52604 2

Editor: Susie Brooks
Designer: Jane Hawkins
Map artwork by Peter Bull
Charts and graph artwork by Encompass Graphics Ltd

Produced for Evans Brothers Limited by
Monkey Puzzle Media Limited
Gissing's Farm, Fressingfield
Suffolk IP21 5SH, UK

All photographs are by David Cumming except *Alamy* 47 bottom (Mediacolors), 57 (Peter Pinnock/ImageState); *Corbis* 55 top (Webistan), 55 bottom (Bojan Brecelj), 56 bottom (Reza/Webistan); *Corbis Digital Stock* front cover lower middle, front and back endpapers; *Eye Ubiquitous* 6–7 (Marcus Wilson Smith), 11 (Marcus Wilson Smith), 13 (Julia Waterlow), 35 bottom (Gary Trotter), 45 top (Steve Lindridge), 49 bottom (Kevin Nicol); *Hutchison Library* 28 bottom (Robin Constable), 44 bottom; *NASA* 15; *Panos Pictures* 22 bottom (Giacomo Pirozzi); *Still Pictures* 23 top (Jorgen Schytte), 28 top (Michael Schwerberger), 36 top (Andreas Buck), 41 bottom (Bojan Brecelj), 43 top (Michael Schwerberger), 43 bottom (Mark Edwards); *Sun World International Inc* 30 both, 31 top.

Endpapers (front): The Sultan Hassan Mosque, seen from the Citadel in Medieval Cairo.
Title page: A street market in Luxor.
Imprint and Contents page: Red Sea mountains in the Eastern Desert.
Endpapers (back): Silhouette of camels alongside the Great Pyramid of Cheops, Giza.

CONTENTS

The Egyptian flag bears the national emblem – a shield superimposed onto the chest of a golden eagle.

The Temple of Hathar at Abu Simbel is one of Egypt's great antiquities.

Egypt is Africa's cultural treasure. Its history stems back to ancient times, and amazing historic buildings still survive. The Nile valley, once home to the world's most advanced civilisation, cuts a lush, fertile ribbon through an otherwise barren landscape. The country occupies an important strategic site, next to the Middle East and across the Mediterranean Sea from Europe.

ANCIENT TIMES

Some 6,000 years ago, the ancient Egyptians were the first people to develop settled agriculture. Their lifeline was the River Nile, which flooded yearly and laid a strip of fertile silt soils across the valley. Despite Egypt's desert climate, this enabled farmers to grow enough crops to feed the entire population.

Egypt is famous for its pyramids, temples and other monuments, built by the ancient Egyptians under their rulers, the pharaohs. There are also cultural legacies from a period of Greek and Roman rule, beginning in AD 322 when Alexander the Great conquered the country. During this era, science, literature and religious teaching became paramount, giving Egypt a world-leading academic profile.

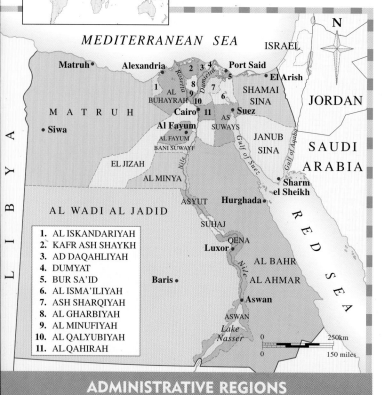

1. AL ISKANDARIYAH
2. KAFR ASH SHAYKH
3. AD DAQAHLIYAH
4. DUMYAT
5. BUR SA'ID
6. AL ISMA'ILIYAH
7. ASH SHARQIYAH
8. AL GHARBIYAH
9. AL MINUFIYAH
10. AL QALYUBIYAH
11. AL QAHIRAH

ADMINISTRATIVE REGIONS

THE ARRIVAL OF ISLAM

An event of great significance to modern Egypt happened in the seventh century AD. Arab Muslims reached the Nile valley, spreading their religion – Islam – to the Egyptian people. From Egypt, Islam continued its spread westwards across the desert belt of north Africa. Modern Egypt is an Arab republic. Islam is the state religion, and Islamic law – known as *sharia* – is apparent in the country's legal system. The majority of Egyptian people are guided by Islam in all aspects of their lives. Egypt is not, however, an Islamic republic like Saudi Arabia. There is also a large minority of Coptic Christians, belonging to the Eastern Orthodox Church.

EUROPEAN INTEREST

During the nineteenth century, interest in Egypt increased from France and Britain. What attracted these countries most was finding a faster route, via Suez, to their empires in Asia. The opening of the Suez Canal in 1869 saved ships the long journey around South Africa's Cape of Good Hope. The British had most to gain from this, and in 1914 Egypt became a British protectorate. Egypt regained independence in 1922, but Britain kept control of defence and the Suez Canal. This ended in 1953 when the modern republic of Egypt was born and the canal was nationalised by the new President Nasser.

This ancient statue of Ramses II, a great pharaoh, remains at Luxor temple.

The Mohammed Ali Mosque, with its distinctive domes and minarets, is a key landmark in Cairo.

POLITICS TODAY

Egypt today, with its large population, is a major player in the Arab world. Part of the country – east of the Suez Canal – lies in the Middle East, a region of great political and military instability. Egypt has tried to be a moderating influence. It has acted as a broker (go-between) in the ongoing conflict between Israel and the Palestinians. The government also tries to maintain good relations with the USA and the European Union (EU). As the most populous Arab country and (after Nigeria) the second most populous in Africa, Egypt is a force that cannot be ignored in world politics.

KEY DATA

Area:	1,001,450km^2
Population:	68.5 million (in 2000)
Capital City:	Cairo
Currency:	Egyptian pound (E£)
GDP Per Capita:	US$3,750*
Highest Point:	Mount St Catherine (2,642m)

*(2001) Calculated on Purchasing Power Parity basis
Source: World Bank

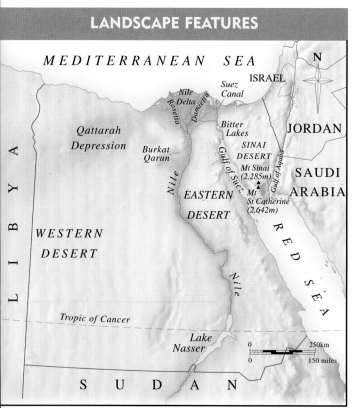

The lush valley of the Nile at Luxor contrasts with the bare desert behind.

Egypt is a desert country. Nowhere within it does the yearly rainfall total more than 250mm, and in many parts significant rain may only come once in five years. Without the life-giving water of the River Nile, the growth and development of ancient and modern civilisations in Egypt would not have been possible. As the Greek philosopher Herodotus wrote, 'Egypt is the gift of the Nile'.

LANDSCAPE FEATURES

MEDITERRANEAN SEA

N

ISRAEL

Suez Canal

Nile Delta

Rosetta

Damietta

Qattarah Depression

Burkat Qarun

Bitter Lakes

JORDAN

SINAI DESERT

Gulf of Suez

Mt Sinai (2,285m)

Gulf of Aqaba

SAUDI ARABIA

Nile

EASTERN DESERT

Mt St Catherine (2,642m)

L I B Y A

WESTERN DESERT

R E D   S E A

Tropic of Cancer

Nile

Lake Nasser

0   250km

0   150 miles

S U D A N

The contrast between the Nile valley and the land it cuts through is striking. A narrow green strip follows the river from Aswan northwards, culminating in a wide triangular delta (see page 15). But this only accounts for about 5 per cent of Egypt's land area. The remaining 95 per cent is covered with sand dunes, loose stones and bare outcrops of rock.

Desert landscapes can be amazing to look at, but they are very difficult to live in. The fierce heat of the daytime sun, from a continuously clear sky, quickly evaporates surface water and dries out plants. Crops soon wilt and die, and settled human life is almost impossible to sustain. Along the Mediterranean coastal strip the desert is partly soil, rather than sand, and some plants will grow there. But elsewhere arid sand and rock prohibit productive agriculture unless major land reclamation work is undertaken (see pages 30–31).

THE WESTERN DESERT

Making up part of Africa's sprawling Sahara Desert, the Western Desert in Egypt is the dry bed of an ancient sea. It is relatively flat with occasional depressions, at the bottom of which supplies of underground fresh water come closer to the surface. Several oases are dotted around as a result. One of the largest, covering some 1,000km^2 is Dakhla, far west of Luxor. Fresh water welling up from deep below the surface allows date palms and other plants to grow here, forming a large patch of green cultivated land between vast expanses of sand. Elsewhere the landscape is dominated by crescent-shaped dunes, called barchans.

CASE STUDY
THE GREAT SAND SEA

Vast desert dunes form an imposing landscape, almost impossible for humans to cross.

The Great Sand Sea stretches for 800km across part of the Western Desert, towards the Libyan border. It is one of the world's last unexplored regions and nothing is able to live there. The outstanding features of this vast red wilderness are crescent-shaped barchans that move slowly across its breadth, carried by prevailing north-east trade winds. The trade winds are continuous because there

THE EASTERN DESERT

To the east of the Nile is a rocky and more mountainous region – on the approach to the Red Sea, summits reach heights of about 750m. To the east of the Red Sea lies the Sinai Desert. Although the Sinai peninsula has fairly flat coastal plains, towards the centre it becomes rugged. Mount St Catherine (2,642m), is the highest peak – but perhaps better known is Mount Sinai (2,285m), where according to the Bible Moses received the Ten Commandments.

In Sinai, loose stones and bare rocks are more common than sand. Wadis are another feature. These are deep, gorge-like valleys, cut into the land by torrents of water that fall with occasional desert thunderstorms. Wadis remain as dried-out channels most of the time, but when there is a downpour, water flows rapidly through them. This creates temporary rivers, teeming with loose rocks and sand.

is no vegetation in the desert to interrupt their flow. They lift sand from the rear of the barchan and blow it up the gentle back slope until it spills over the steep face of the dune – hence the sand is in almost constant motion and the dunes keep changing their positions. The amount of sand at the sides of the barchans is less than that in the centre, so the sides are driven forwards more quickly, forming narrow horns at the leading edges.

Because of the constant winds, anyone who attempts to make a track or build a road through the Great Sand Sea must be prepared to maintain it with regular use of sand ploughs. Travel can be extremely difficult and dangerous in the Western Desert. Where it is possible, camels are a more useful means of transport than vehicles because they can negotiate the dunes without the need for beaten paths.

A DESERT CLIMATE

Egypt is one of the driest, hottest and sunniest countries in the world. It is said to have a desert climate, which means it experiences an average annual rainfall of less than 250mm. The wettest part of Egypt is along the Mediterranean coastal strip, but none of the weather stations there have recorded more than 200mm of rain in a single year.

RAINFALL

Most of Egypt lies within the Sahara Desert. Here, high pressure dominates – in other words, air mostly sinks in the atmosphere. The Sahara lies between 20° and 30° north of the Equator in a high pressure belt. As part of the world pattern of pressure and winds, air that has risen at the Equator flows at high levels in the atmosphere towards the poles. Some of this air sinks over the Sahara Desert. The sinking air stops air currents from the ground, heated by the hot surface, from rising to high levels in the atmosphere. Only by reaching high levels could they cool down sufficiently for moisture in the air to condense and form clouds and rain.

A little more rain falls in places along the Mediterranean coast – such as Alexandria – mainly in winter. This is caused by frontal depressions (areas of low pressure where air currents rise). They move from west to east through the Mediterranean Sea in winter, bringing variable weather with some cloudy and wet days. These conditions are very unusual further south in Egypt, where high pressure dominates in winter as well. In southern Egypt, several years may pass before any real rainfall is recorded.

TEMPERATURE AND RAINFALL

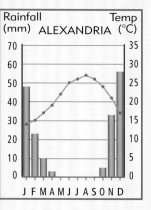

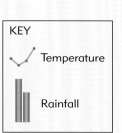

KEY

Temperature

Rainfall

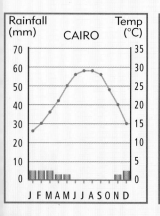

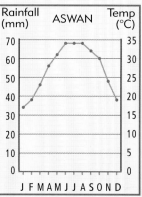

Tourists provide a vital income for many Bedouins who cannot earn a living from farming in the arid, barren desert.

TEMPERATURE

Egypt's summer heat is fierce. Daytime temperatures of between 45°C and 50°C are common, and that is in the shade! There is no relief from the summer heat in central and southern Egypt – the sun shines from a high angle through cloudless skies. However, humidity is very low, which makes the heat more bearable than it might sound. At night, surface heat is lost quickly due to clear skies. Winter nights are cool everywhere in Egypt – temperatures often fall to 5°C or less, though icy temperatures of below 0°C are very rare.

The worst weather occurs when a hot, dry wind – known as the *khamsin* (meaning '50 days') – blows. This happens most in spring and early summer. The wind feels like the blast of heat that hits you when you open the door of a hot oven. Temperatures can climb to dangerously high levels. As the wind whips over desert surfaces, it heats up and fills with dust particles. These cut down the visibility to zero and can remove paint from cars, scratch windscreens and disrupt air traffic at Cairo's international airport. In many areas it is almost impossible for people to stay outside during the *khamsin* because the dust irritates the eyes, nose and mouth.

Egypt's best weather comes in winter. Away from the Mediterranean coast, the daytime climate in this season is ideal for holiday-makers – constantly dry and sunny without being too hot. Typical maximum temperatures are between 20°C and 25°C. It is like good summer weather in the UK – but it is more reliable, occurring consistently every winter.

EGYPT'S CLIMATE: ADVANTAGES AND DISADVANTAGES

ADVANTAGES

- Sunny and hot so that, with irrigation, plants will grow all year round.
- Guaranteed warm and sunny winters, ideal for visitors.
- Low humidity, making summer heat easier to bear.

DISADVANTAGES

- Nowhere has enough rain for crops to grow without irrigation.
- Water is lost quickly through evaporation in the extreme summer heat.
- Fierce summer temperatures and dusty desert winds hinder farming and travelling and deter visitors.

Small towns, like this one at Farafra, have grown up around occasional desert oases whose water makes life possible despite the lack of rainfall.

Near Aswan, the Nile valley is so narrow that the desert almost touches the river.

THE RIVER NILE

One statistic puts the River Nile in all the record books – its length. From the source of its most southerly tributary (almost on the Equator), to its furthest distributary at the Mediterranean Sea, it measures more than 6,400km. This makes it the world's longest river. Approximately the last 1,000km of the Nile passes through Egypt.

The Nile has two sources. The branch that gives the river its great length is the White Nile, which flows from Lake Victoria, high in the mountains of Uganda. Here the climate is equatorial – wet all year round. The White Nile supplies approximately the same amount of water every month.

The Blue Nile is the branch of the Nile that, until the building of the Aswan High Dam (see page 16), flooded naturally every summer. The Blue Nile's source is Lake Tana in the highlands of Ethiopia, which receives heavy summer monsoon rains. Estimates suggest that 85 per cent of the water used in Egypt comes originally from the Blue Nile.

The Blue Nile meets the White Nile at Khartoum in Sudan. For the last 2,700km of its course through Sudan and Egypt, the Nile has no tributaries and receives very little rainfall.

THE NILE VALLEY

Egyptians divide their section of the Nile valley into two parts – Upper Egypt in the south and Lower Egypt in the north. This relates to the way geographers call the source end of rivers the upper course, and the latter end the lower course.

UPPER EGYPT

In Upper Egypt, the Nile flows in places over hard outcrops of rock. Here, the river valley is narrow. The water mainly cuts downwards (vertical erosion) because it is unable to erode sideways (lateral erosion) into the impenetrable cliffs. Rocky gorges have formed and sections of the channel are dominated by small waterfalls and rapids. These form dangerous 'cataracts' that have famously caused problems for boats trying to navigate the full length of the Nile in Egypt.

LOWER EGYPT AND THE DELTA

In Lower Egypt, rocks are softer and the Nile has been able to form a broader valley, on average some 10km wide. The river itself averages 800m across. The Nile meanders (bends) back and forth across its floodplain through the desert.

Between Cairo and the Mediterranean Sea, the river changes character. North of Cairo it splits into many separate channels, known as distributaries. These include two major branches – the River Damietta and the River Rosetta. The land spanned by the distributaries is called the Nile Delta – it is a triangular area of flat terrain, shaped like the Greek symbol for D (Δ: delta), hence its name. As the river nears the sea, its flow slows down and silt suspended in the water sinks to the bottom. From ancient times, Nile silt deposited on the floor of the Mediterranean Sea built up until it rose above sea level and formed new land – the delta – at the coast.

Every time the Nile flooded, its distributaries also spread a new layer of fertile silt on to the flooded land surface. As a result, the Nile Delta is one of the world's most productive farming areas. During hundreds of thousands of years the Nile has deposited so much silt that the delta today measures more than 200km between Cairo, at its southern point, and Alexandria on the western side.

This satellite image shows the course of the Nile valley through Egypt. The triangular delta is the broadest area of green land in the country.

This Nilometer was used to keep a strict check on the rise and fall of water levels in the river.

MANAGING THE NILE

Water sustains life. This is true everywhere in the world, but it is most apparent in desert regions where moisture is severely lacking. In terms of rainfall, Egypt is one of the world's driest countries. However, due to the north-bound flow of the River Nile, Egypt benefits from rainwater that falls in Ethiopia and the tropics further south. Without the Nile, Egypt could not support a fraction of the population it maintains today. Egyptians need to ensure that their life-giving supply is conserved.

In ancient times, the Egyptians measured the height of the Nile flood in Cairo to predict their harvest and determine the taxes for the following year – a low flood meant less irrigation and silt, poor crops and starvation.

Today there is more control. The Egyptian stretch of the Nile is now a managed river – it is no longer allowed to flood naturally. National water supplies are distributed from the Aswan High Dam and Lake Nasser in the south, and numerous small canals dispense water to a patchwork of cultivated fields.

THE ASWAN HIGH DAM

The Aswan High Dam is a large-scale, multi-purpose river management scheme. Building it was a great feat of engineering. Everything about the dam is huge – it is 3.6km long, 111m high and contains sufficient concrete and stone to have built another 20 of the Great Pyramids (see page 46). It was begun in 1960 and completed in 1971, using aid and engineering expertise from the Soviet Union.

The dam holds back Lake Nasser, named after the first president of the modern republic of Egypt who ensured that the project went ahead. At the time the lake was the largest artificial reservoir in the world. It measures 500km in length and stretches beyond the southern border of Egypt into Sudan. It looks like a large inland sea, surrounded by desert.

The Aswan High Dam is one of the world's largest river management constructions.

The main reason for constructing the dam and lake was to control and store the flood-waters of the Nile. By doing this, for the first time in the history of Egypt, water could be conserved and released as and when it was needed. This made more water available to farmers in the dry season, allowing them to irrigate two or more crops per year. The dam had other benefits, too, such as freedom from the dangers of flooding, and the possibility of hydroelectric power (HEP).

A CONTROVERSIAL PROJECT

The Aswan High Dam is generally hailed as the key to the modernisation of Egypt, allowing the country economic development. However, it sparked controversy at the time it was built. Local people were forced to move from land that they had lived on for thousands of years,

Surrounded by desert sands, Lake Nasser stores around 170,000km^3 of water from the Nile.

and the ancient Abu Simbel temples had to be relocated (see page 49). The cost of the whole scheme was phenomenal. Could a poor country like Egypt afford such a large dam?

Since its construction, the dam has been blamed for some serious environmental and economic problems. Silt is now trapped behind the dam; in time Lake Nasser will begin to silt up. Each year some 20 per cent of the lake's water is lost through seepage and evaporation, and fertile soil has stopped being deposited across the floor of the Nile valley. This is having a detrimental effect on local farmers (see page 29). Cairo brickmakers have also suffered as they no longer have a ready supply of river mud to make their bricks.

CASE STUDY
THE NILE BASIN INITIATIVE (NBI)

The rivers of the Nile basin flow through ten vastly different countries between the heart of Africa and the Mediterranean Sea. For many years, pressure from rising populations, along with limited access to Nile water, has increased the chances of conflict between them. In 1959, Sudan and Egypt agreed to share out the Nile water on a quota system. However, Ethiopia refused to sign this arrangement and there has been tension between the countries ever since.

Ethiopia is a key country, because its rains supply so much of the water that fills the Blue Nile in summer. Also, Ethiopia badly needs access to more water, having suffered several major droughts since the 1970s. Egypt recognises its own vulnerable position, because the Nile water reaches it last.

The ten countries in the Nile basin have now come to realise that it is in all of their interests to co-operate. They are hoping to find ways of:
• making available the greatest possible amount of water
• sharing out the stored resources fairly.

This co-operation is being manifested in the Nile Basin Initiative (NBI). In 2001, funding of US$140 million was secured from the World Bank and donor governments to finance seven feasibility studies. Officials are in the process of setting up a legal framework so that there can be no future disagreements. One study is being carried out in the highlands of Ethiopia, where the mountainous landscape is favourable for building dams and the cooler air means there is less risk of evaporation from stored water. Preserving supplies here, at the river's source, is one way of increasing the amount of water available to all ten countries in the Nile basin.

POPULATION

People crowd the streets of Cairo, now one of the world's largest cities.

Egypt's population has three outstanding features – firstly, most people live within 100km of the River Nile; secondly, the population has grown rapidly in the last 50 years, creating many problems; and thirdly, the majority of Egyptians are Muslim, living by the Islamic faith.

POPULATION CLUSTERS

The population of Egypt is very unevenly distributed. Most of its 68.5 million people live on just 5 per cent of the land, forming a narrow strip that follows the River Nile. The rest of the country is largely uninhabited desert – the Great Sand Sea in the west is one of the emptiest places on the Earth's surface. People and settlements cluster around a small number of oases, which are the only spots where fresh water is naturally available or can be supplied to support life. Elsewhere in the desert, a few nomadic Bedouin groups cling to a traditional existence. They are constantly on the move, searching for grazing for their herds of camels and goats. However, their numbers are small and they are now being encouraged to settle in permanent villages in the desert.

POPULATION DENSITY

The average population density in Egypt is 86 people per square kilometre – but average figures mean little, considering 95 per cent of the country's land area is uninhabited. The lower Nile valley is one of the world's most densely populated areas, yet to the east and west of it the reverse is true.

Small Bedouin groups make temporary camps in Egypt's vast and largely empty desert.

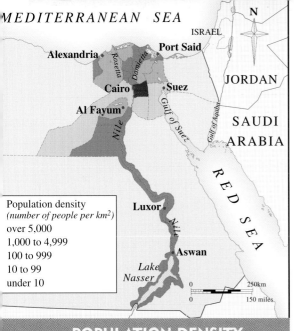

Population density
(number of people per km²)
over 5,000
1,000 to 4,999
100 to 999
10 to 99
under 10

POPULATION DENSITY

In rural areas, high densities centre around agriculture in the Nile valley and delta, where two or three crops a year can now be grown in the same field. High yields of cereals and vegetables are obtained from the fertile soils, providing food for large numbers of people.

All of Egypt's major urban areas are located in the Nile valley as well. Population densities are highest of all in central Cairo, which is chronically overcrowded. New arrivals from the countryside have increased the density by making their homes in every bit of available space, including rooftops and tombs in cemeteries (see page 33). It is estimated that more than 20 million people – up to one-third of the Egyptian population – live in Cairo and Alexandria alone. These are Egypt's two largest cities, and both continue to grow.

URBAN POPULATION

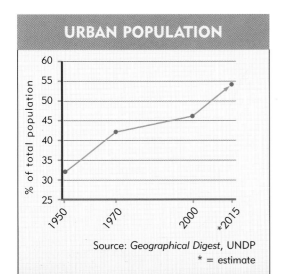

Source: *Geographical Digest*, UNDP
* = estimate

CASE STUDY
RURAL TO URBAN MIGRATION

Many wealthy businessmen operate in Cairo, where Egypt's best-paid jobs are concentrated.

Migration from the countryside to the cities is happening on a massive scale in Egypt. It can be explained by a mixture of push and pull factors.

The main push factor from rural areas is population pressure in the old agricultural zones. As families have become larger, the amount of farmland and food output per head has reduced. Also, poverty is greater in the villages than in the towns, and rural settlements have fewer services such as schools and clinics.

The main pull factor to urban areas is work. Types of employment are more varied here than in the countryside. Wage rates, although low by developed world standards, are higher as well. In addition, the cities offer more opportunities for education and gaining new skills.

The large gap in wealth between countryside and cities is widening rather than narrowing. So despite the problems that this one-way migration is creating (see pages 34–35), there is little chance that it will slow down or stop in the forseeable future.

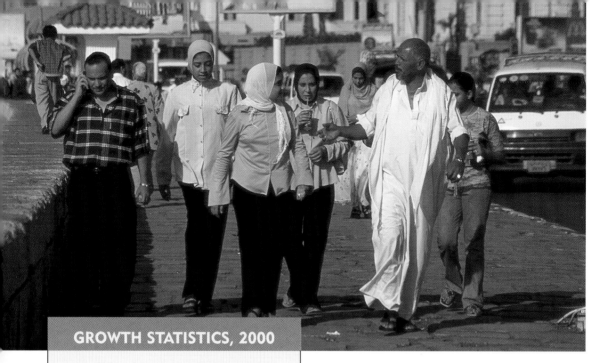

GROWTH STATISTICS, 2000

Birth Rate	25 per 1,000 people
Death Rate	7 per 1,000 people
Natural Increase	18 per 1,000 people (or 1.8%) per year

Source: UNDP

POPULATION GROWTH

As in other developing countries in Africa and the Middle East, population growth in Egypt has been rapid over the last 50 years. The total population more than doubled between 1970 and 2000, and it is still growing by more than one million people per year.

Population growth occurs when birth rates exceed death rates. The difference between the two figures is called the natural increase.

REASONS FOR GROWTH

Several factors contribute to Egypt's high birth rate, and hence to its population growth.

Firstly, the family remains at the centre of Egyptian life. Egyptians value children very highly. In rural areas they are useful workers, both on the farm and in the home. They are also a great source of security for ageing parents – governments in less economically developed countries cannot afford the pension and social security schemes that rich European countries provide for their elderly.

Families are traditionally much larger in Egypt than in the UK. Couples need to have fewer children if population growth is to be controlled.

There is another important cultural reason. Islam states that a Muslim man may have four wives, or even more, provided he can afford to support them and their offspring, and assuming he treats them all equally. This means he is likely to father more children. Also, many strict Muslims believe that the Islamic religion does not tolerate the use of contraception, an attitude that again leads to increased family size.

Early marriages, young parents and large families are old traditions in Egypt, and they are proving hard to break. In 2003, 40 per cent of Egyptians were under 13 years old.

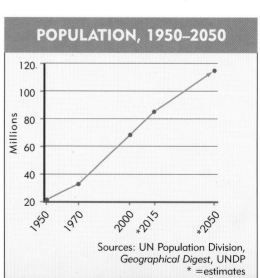

POPULATION, 1950–2050

Sources: UN Population Division, *Geographical Digest*, UNDP
* =estimates

So Egypt cannot hope to escape further population growth immediately because there will be a high proportion of people reaching child-bearing ages for many years to come.

The dramatic fall in Egypt's death rate has been another important factor. This is largely due to vast improvements in healthcare, which also explain the figures for life expectancy. In 1960 the life expectancy for a newly born Egyptian was only 46 years; now it is more than 65 years. With more people surviving to old age, the population continues to grow.

POPULATION PROBLEMS

A higher food output is needed to feed the increasing millions in Egypt, but the delta region is already farmed to its full potential, and expanding the area of agricultural land is a slow and expensive process (see page 30).

By 2003, more than 900,000 young people a year were leaving schools and universities to find jobs. Just to stop unemployment increasing, a similar number of new jobs needed to be created every year. The economy was not growing fast enough for this to happen, so the unemployment rate has escalated (see also page 53). To create jobs for all these people the economy would need to expand by 7 per cent per year. Most experts agree that government targets for growth of about 5 per cent per year are unlikely to be achieved because there is no sign of the massive investment from overseas companies that would be needed for this to happen.

Even the new highways in Cairo are congested as a result of persistent population growth.

The problem of unemployment is most serious in the countryside, where farming is often the only type of work available. Lack of work is fuelling the mass movement of young people into urban areas, so problems are being transferred from the countryside to the cities. Rapid growth is worsening existing urban problems such as housing shortages, inadequate and over-stretched public services, chronic traffic congestion, and water and atmospheric pollution (see pages 34–35).

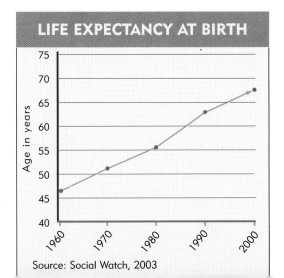

LIFE EXPECTANCY AT BIRTH

Source: Social Watch, 2003

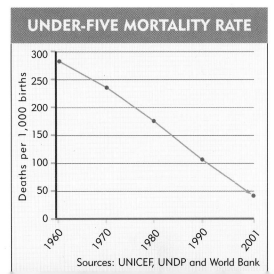

UNDER-FIVE MORTALITY RATE

Sources: UNICEF, UNDP and World Bank

FAMILY PLANNING

On the positive side, the birth rate in Egypt is falling. More than 20 years of government-backed family planning campaigns, supported by overseas aid, are beginning to take effect. At least half of the married women in Egypt now use some form of birth control.

Uptake has been greatest among urban inhabitants. People living in big cities have received a higher level of education and are usually in a better position to change their lifestyles than those in the countryside. Rural dwellers tend to maintain their traditions for longer. Also, children are more obviously useful for labour around the farm than they are in an urban environment.

However, in rural areas close to the big cities, the outlook is changing fast. A son is no longer expected to automatically take a share in his father's land; education is being viewed as more important. Poor farmers are borrowing money to offer their sons the chance to receive academic training. If the son can eventually gain a well-paid job in the city, or even overseas, the whole family stands to benefit. This represents a massive switch in attitude compared with 20 years ago.

Attitude is important, but it is not all that matters. One survey showed that up to 25 per cent of women in rural areas wanted to stop having children but did not use a method of birth control. This was due to lack of easy access to contraception. The government priority, in order to reduce the birth rate further, is to target women living in more remote rural areas. They are the ones with the least formal education and are the most likely to marry and have children when young.

AVERAGE NUMBER OF CHILDREN PER FAMILY

Source: UN Population Division

Health workers distribute family planning information in villages where birth rates are high.

THE VALUE OF EDUCATION

The Egyptian government is committed
to providing free education for all, up to
university level. In the five years from 1996
to 2001, two new schools were being started
every day. The government knows that women
who work and start a career are more likely to
want smaller families. They need to convince

Education is opening up new opportunities
to children throughout rural Egypt.

people of this – but changing old customs
and attitudes in the rural areas of an Islamic
country is not easy. Here, the traditional role
of a woman in society is very different from
that in Western countries (see page 25).

Children are highly valued in Egypt, but many
Egyptian women wish to limit their family size.

CASE STUDY
HODA'S VIEW ON BIRTH CONTROL

'My name is Hoda; I am 30 years old and I live
in Cairo. I have five children, but I want no
more. That's why I've recently been to the
family planning clinic. My 21-year-old sister
came with me as well. She has two daughters
and feels that is enough. Her husband would
like a son, but he is not putting too much
pressure on her. We cannot afford to clothe,
feed or house any more children.

'I am a devout Muslim. I am convinced that
Islam is not against family planning and I know
the government believes this. But my brother-
in-law is a strict religious man and he orders
his wife not to use contraception. He has tried
to persuade me, but I ignore him. I encourage
all my friends to come to the clinic so that
they are aware of the options available to
them. I think we should all have the chance
to choose the extent of our own families.'

Prayer time on the streets of Cairo. Muslim worship may take place anywhere, not just in the mosque.

THE MUSLIM MAJORITY

About 90 per cent of Egyptians are Muslims. They believe in the revelations of the Prophet Mohammed, as written in their holy book, the Koran. No village, however small, is without a mosque – in most towns and villages, characteristic domes and minarets dominate the skyline, and for big cities such as Cairo, mosques are among the main landmarks.

All visitors to Egypt are quickly aware that they are visiting an Islamic country. The voice of the *muezzin* (religious caller) can be heard everywhere, five times a day, chanting a standard prayer that calls the faithful to worship. At prayer times, mats are laid out in the most unusual places – for example on platforms at railway stations or next to roads in the middle of the desert. Daytime scenes are quieter than usual during the month of Ramadan, when adults refrain from eating and drinking during daylight hours; but after sunset, the streets come alive with people feasting and enjoying open-air festivities.

Traditional robes cover the full body and feet.

ASPECTS OF EGYPTIAN LIF

RELIGION – THE 5 PILLARS OF FAITH FOR EVERY GOOD MUSLIM

- Faith – 'There is no God but Allah and Mohammed is His Prophet'.

- Prayer – to be said at five specific times every day, facing Mecca.

- Fasting – during daylight hours in the month of Ramadan.

- Pilgrimage – a holy journey to Mecca in Saudi Arabia, to be made at least once in a lifetime.

- Charity – paying a religious levy (tax) to help the ill or poor.

LANGUAGE – ARABIC

- Writing and reading of Arabic script is from right to left.

- Books are read from back to front.

- Useful phrases in Arabic include:
  Inshallah – God willing
  Shokran – Thank you
  Baksheesh – Share the wealth
  (also the term used for a tip).

TRADITIONAL DRESS

- The *galabiyeh* – a full-length robe, like a nightshirt.

- A turban-like headcloth or skullcap for men.

- A coloured or black headscarf for women, sometimes with a veil.

Traditional Islamic society is male dominated. Men are responsible for working and earning money to support their wives and children, while women are expected to be in charge of the home, bringing up the children. In some Muslim countries women are not allowed to leave the house without being accompanied by their husbands. The roles of men and women are separated much more strictly than in Western countries.

Egyptian society as a whole takes a more relaxed view than many other Islamic nations. Women are not segregated from everyday life or forced to wear the veil, even in villages in the countryside where Islamic traditions remain strongest. In the cities, they will travel in the same coaches on trains as men, although there are always separate women-only coaches available on trains and the Cairo metro (see page 36). Despite this, men still dominate the work-force. This contrasts with the UK where there are almost as many female workers as male workers, even if, due to family commitments, a higher proportion of females work part-time.

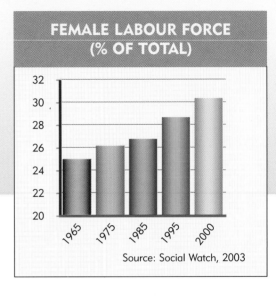

FEMALE LABOUR FORCE (% OF TOTAL)

Source: Social Watch, 2003

THE COPTIC MINORITY

Aside from Muslims, most of the remaining 10 per cent of Egyptians are Coptic Christians. They claim to be direct descendants of the ancient Egyptians, and their name derives from the Greek word for an ancient Egyptian. Coptic Christians have maintained their own language and customs and their churches have crosses, which makes them easy to recognise. Christian festivals such as Christmas and Easter are major celebrations, although the Coptic Christmas takes place on 6th January. The Copts have links to the Greek Orthodox Church, but remain separate from Western Christian groups, such as the Roman Catholics. In Wadi Natron in the Western Desert, several Coptic monasteries are being redeveloped with financial support from city-dwelling Copts. Tensions between Copts and Muslims do exist, sometimes surfacing with destructive or violent acts, and the government is under pressure to promote harmony (see page 52). But the two groups have co-existed for centuries and most Egyptian Muslims are quite relaxed about religion, even though it is very important to them.

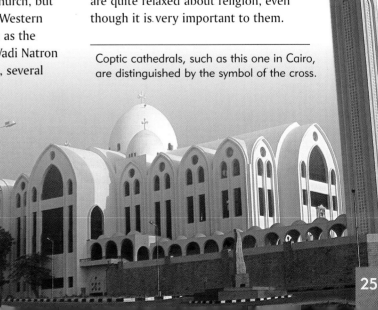

Coptic cathedrals, such as this one in Cairo, are distinguished by the symbol of the cross.

Children and animals are regular workers on most Egyptian farms.

Farming in the Nile valley has been an essential activity for 6,000 years. It remains very important in Egypt today, although its role is declining compared to many other industries. In such a dry country, agriculture is only possible with irrigation.

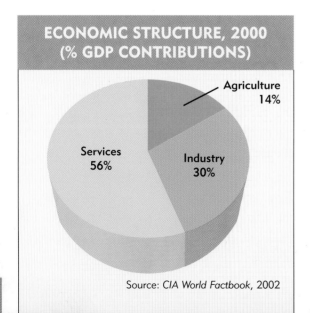

ECONOMIC STRUCTURE, 2000 (% GDP CONTRIBUTIONS)

Agriculture 14%

Services 56%

Industry 30%

Source: *CIA World Factbook*, 2002

A VITAL INDUSTRY

The continuing importance of farming in Egypt reveals itself in employment statistics. Up to one-third of the labour force are farmers and farm workers, so for at least 15 million Egyptians, the land is their main source of income. Agriculture accounts for 14 per cent of the national GDP (compared to 1 per cent in Germany, for example). It provides the country's second most important export – cotton – which is also the main raw material for textiles, Egypt's largest manufacturing industry.

THE NILE VALLEY: FAVOURABLE CONDITIONS FOR FARMING

- Soils are generally deep, easy to work and fertile.
- Weather is hot and sunny, giving a year-round growing season for crops provided water is available.
- The big climatic problem – minimal rainfall – is overcome by the availability of water from the River Nile.

TRADITIONAL FARMING METHODS

The majority of peasant farmers, called *fellahin*, still work the fertile soils of the Nile valley in much the same way as their ancient ancestors did. Cows and oxen can be seen pulling wooden ploughs in small fields. The grain is harvested using hand sickles (curved knives) and the whole family helps to tie the harvested crop in bundles and carry it to the threshing floor. Men from the village thresh the grain by beating it and throwing it up into the wind to separate the grain from the straw. Threshing was done like this in Biblical times. So many aspects of farming in rural Egypt have not changed for centuries.

Most peasant farmers have no more than 1 hectare of land from which to supply food for themselves and their families. On tiny plots they grow a mixture of cereals – mainly wheat and maize – and vegetables, such as beans, peas and onions. Many spend a large proportion of their working lives lifting water into irrigation channels, and then opening and closing the channels between the plots. The main growing season is between June and October, but now that water is available all year, a second crop is usually grown in the cooler months between November and May. These farmers do not have enough money or

Cutting sugar cane with a hand sickle is slow, back-breaking work in the harsh Egyptian heat.

resources to grow three crops a year, as large commercial cultivators can afford to do.

FARMING IN DECLINE

While agriculture remains significant in Egypt, its role is also declining. Long gone are the days when farming employed over 80 per cent of the workforce. Mechanisation of farming cuts the time required for planting and harvesting and lessens the demand for manual labour in these activities. Now about half of the people in Egypt are urban dwellers, many of whom have never set foot on a farm. Due to increasing demands from Egypt's growing population, the percentage value of agricultural exports is the lowest ever. Crop yields are insufficient and about half of the wheat needed for making bread – a staple food for most Egyptians – has to be imported. The country is now a long way from being self-sufficient in its main foodstuffs.

Local farmers use a *shaduf* to raise water from the river into a network of irrigation channels.

IRRIGATING THE LAND

The ancient Egyptians were world experts on irrigation. They built water channels that criss-crossed and separated small fields, and they invented three methods of lifting water from the rivers and channels into the fields – these were the *shaduf*, the water wheel (*sakia*) and the Archimedean screw (see case study below).

CONTROLLING THE FLOOD

Due to population increase over the centuries, demands for more, and more reliable, supplies of water have grown. Although nature once did a good job during the Nile flood by watering the land and leaving fertile mud behind, the amount of floodwater was not the same every year. This made life very difficult for farmers. Sometimes the flood was so severe that banks between fields were washed away; at other times the flood arrived late, with water levels too low to reach all the irrigation channels.

CASE STUDY
ANCIENT METHODS OF IRRIGATION

The *sakia* turns as the cow walks round; the scoops lift up water and tip it into a channel.

The *shaduf* is a lever system in which a pole is balanced across a horizontal support. On one end of the pole hangs a bucket. At the other end, a weight enables the bucket to be lifted easily when it is full of water.

The *sakia* is a large wheel with scoops around its edge for lifting water. It operates using a cog system and is driven by an animal, usually a cow or an ox in Egypt.

The Archimedean screw is a hand-turned cylinder with a screw inside that draws up water, operating rather like a drill.

The first two of these methods are still widely used today, not only in Egypt but also in other parts of Africa and the Middle East. They remain effective, but they are small-scale, allowing only a limited amount of water to be lifted onto the land. However, compared to a large-scale scheme such as the Aswan High Dam, they are environmentally friendly. What's more, poor farmers can afford to use them – simple technology means that they can repair and maintain them effectively. In other words, they are examples of appropriate technology, because they are cheap and reliable and there is little to go wrong. What they cannot do is greatly increase the extent of irrigated farmland.

During the nineteenth and early twentieth centuries, a number of barrages were built across the river to store floodwater for use later in the year. The largest of these was the old dam at Aswan, built in the 1930s – but it was not large enough to control the Nile flood and to supply water everywhere in the valley, all the time. This only became possible when the Aswan High Dam was completed in 1971.

In the Nile Delta, river flow has now been confined to just two main channels. It is from these that water is drawn to irrigate Egypt's best farmland. The large delta farms (over 50 hectares) grow Egypt's main cash crop, cotton, which is renowned throughout the world for its quality (see page 43). Nile water is also taken to oases away from the valley. One of these is at Al Fayum, about 100km south-west of Cairo. Here, a natural reservoir in a desert depression – Lake Qarun – is kept filled by Nile water. In turn this has allowed a great increase in the extent of cultivated land.

EFFECTS OF MAJOR IRRIGATION

As we've seen (on page 17), the High Dam brought tremendous advantages to farmers. Yields of maize, rice, cotton and sugar cane increased dramatically and the cultivated area of Egypt doubled from 4 per cent to 8 per cent. However, the silt that once arrived with the flood is now trapped behind the dam wall and is not available for the land. As a result, artificial fertilisers are increasingly required to produce crops of sufficient quality and quantity. Fertilisers are expensive for poor farmers to buy, and the chemicals in them pollute underground and surface water. The many irrigation channels also increase the number of breeding sites for bilharzia snails. Bilharzia is a dangerous disease among farmers in the Nile valley – it severely weakens those who catch it and can be fatal.

Another problem encountered in all irrigated areas is salination – an unhealthy build-up of salts in the surface soils. When crops are irrigated, some of the water is lost through evaporation. In Egypt, large amounts of irrigation water are applied year-round because otherwise no crops can grow – and rates of evaporation are consistently high because of the great daytime heat. Evaporation draws underground salts up to the surface of the soil. This salination process kills crops, reduces yields and renders the soil unsuitable for further planting. The problem can be reduced, although not totally avoided, if water is supplied directly to the area around the crop roots. In this way a higher percentage of water is used up by the plant before it can evaporate.

The Damietta Dam helps to control river levels and supply water to farms in the Nile Delta.

FUTURE FARMING

Aside from the physical problems posed by the Aswan High Dam, the main difficulties faced by Egypt's farmers are economic ones.

Agriculture in Egypt is in urgent need of modernisation to increase output and efficiency. But this is a difficult task in a country of peasant farmers who work tiny plots of land, just 1 or 2 hectares in size. These farmers are too poor to invest in new seeds and equipment, and many are reluctant to adopt modern techniques.

Larger farms, up to 100 hectares in size, are usually operated more commercially. However, their owners complain about government interference. The government is eager to find ways of increasing farm yields, in order to reduce the country's reliance upon imported foods. Skills in marketing and packaging food products are in short supply in Egypt, which is one of the reasons why food importers have found it easy to enter the Egyptian market. The Egyptian government's preferred line of action is to reclaim more land from the desert and fill it with new crops.

LAND RECLAMATION

The government's big hope is to turn the red desert sands into giant oases of green cultivation. It has been described as 'dreaming of making another California'. Two major projects are going ahead – the South Valley Development Project in the south-west of the country (see case study opposite), and the Northern Sinai Development Project in the north-east. The overall aim is very ambitious – to increase the land area under cultivation by 40 per cent, from 3 million to 5 million hectares. Both projects are similar in that they depend upon canals being built to transfer Nile water further into the desert than ever before.

LEFT: Reclaiming desert land allows more crops, such as these grapes, to be grown for export.
BELOW: The Sheik Zayed Canal under construction. It was built to channel Nile water to reclaimed land in the southern desert.

COUNTING THE COSTS

For a relatively poor country like Egypt, with a weak economy, the cost of these schemes is enormous. The government is already talking in terms of hundreds of millions of dollars – and prices invariably increase with time, far exceeding original estimates. The government of Egypt could not have begun the schemes without financial help from oil-rich Arab states such as Saudi Arabia, Kuwait and Dubai. Most of the money needed, however, will have to come from within Egypt.

Constructing major land reclamation facilities, such as this pumping station at Tushka (hub of the South Valley scheme) is highly expensive.

Some people think that the government's plans are too big and too ambitious (see page 54). Also, is there enough water available from the Nile to make the projects sustainable? The answer to this will depend upon the amount of water Egypt is allocated when the NBI (see page 17) is fully operational. As yet, it is unclear when this will be.

(see page 54)

(see page 17)

CASE STUDY
THE SOUTH VALLEY DEVELOPMENT PROJECT

The eventual aim of the South Valley Development Project is to build a canal 300km long, carrying Nile water from Lake Nasser to the desert oasis of Baris. The powerhouse for the scheme is the world's largest pumping station at Tushka on the western shore of Lake Nasser.

The first phase of the project was more modest – building the 30km Sheik Zayed Canal, from which half a million hectares of land can be irrigated and cultivated. Experimental planting of crops in this area began in 1999. As soon as the pumping station was working in late 2002, water began to flow in the canal and the first attempt to reclaim some 4,000 hectares of desert began. The largest private investment is by the Saudi Arabian company Kadco (Kingdom Agricultural Development Company), which bought one of the first four blocks of land. They have passed irrigation water underground to allow vineyards of grapes to be grown. The company is looking for a 20 per cent return on its investment. If this is achieved after a few years of operation, other investors will be encouraged to follow. Investment by individuals and companies has been encouraged by offers of low land rents and the chance of 20 years of income without paying tax. The hope is to bring the desert to life with fields of cotton, and crops that can be sold in Europe during winter, including grapes, citrus fruits and tomatoes.

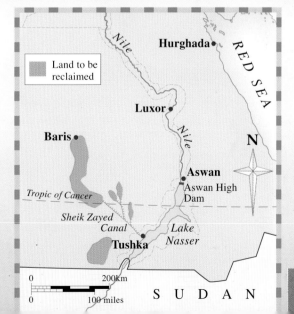

Cairo is a sprawling mixture of old, new, traditional and modern architecture.

Cairo and Alexandria are Egypt's two main urban centres. Cairo is one of the world's most populous cities. It acts like a magnet, drawing in people from all over Egypt, but great growth has caused serious long-term problems. Alexandria is smaller than Cairo, so difficulties here occur on a lesser scale. Nevertheless, it exemplifies troubles that exist throughout urban Egypt.

COLOSSAL CAIRO

Cairo is more than 1,000 years old, one of the world's oldest cities. It is also classed as a 'mega city' (having in excess of 10 million inhabitants). Its population is estimated to be at least 16 million, perhaps 20 million, making it the largest city in Africa and the Arab world. Growth is estimated at 300,000 people a year, mainly due to migration from the countryside. Cairo is Egypt's most powerful urban magnet because it has the widest range of job opportunities. Also, it is the nation's capital city and houses the main government offices.

Visitors to Cairo may wonder why the city is so attractive to immigrants. The streets teem with people and the main roads are choked by traffic all day long. Donkey-drawn carts do battle with cars for space on unnervingly narrow side streets. The noise is horrendous and air pollution reaches dangerous levels on many days of the year. But despite the apparent chaos, Cairo is a dynamic city, driven by energetic inhabitants and animated with a rich and vibrant culture.

ADVANTAGES OF LIVING IN CAIRO

	CAIRO	RURAL EGYPT
Income per Year (Egyptian £)	3,460	2,350
Infant Mortality Rate (per 1,000)	50	68

(Average figures)

Source: Egyptian Government

THE LAYOUT OF CAIRO

Dividing Cairo into distinctive zones is not easy because there has been little urban planning. Old and new are often found side by side. Vast modern flyovers loop around medieval mosques, while luxury penthouses and apartment blocks tower above crumbling mud brick shacks.

Central Cairo lies on the east bank of the River Nile. The waterfront is lined with tall buildings – many quite modern – built mainly of concrete and glass. The majority of these are used for offices; some are hotels. This area, however, is not the main place of work in Cairo.

Most employment activity takes place further east, in the old quarter of medieval Cairo – an area of narrow lanes and alleys. At ground level there are rows of tiny, tightly-packed workshops and shops, above which cramped apartments pile up, with people living at every level up to and including the roof. This is the zone with the highest incidence of mosques, of which the best known is El-Azhar, the leading centre of Islamic learning in Egypt (see page 47). About a kilometre further east are the 'Cities of the Dead' – a derelict cemetery area where many of the capital's poorest people live in and among the old tombs.

New residential districts for wealthy inhabitants have been built on the western and eastern sides of Cairo, on land that was formerly desert. These prosperous-looking suburbs of mansions and villas have names associated more with the USA than with Egypt, such as 'Sunset Hills' and 'Dreamland'.

Tiny workshops like this cobbler's are tightly crammed into the streets of old Cairo.

Dreamland is a complex of luxury apartments, fringed by greenery on reclaimed desert land.

URBAN PROBLEMS IN CAIRO

Cairo's urban problems are similar to those suffered by other mega cities around the world. The four most glaring concerns are overcrowded and poor-quality housing, inadequate provision of public services, traffic congestion leading to air pollution, and urban sprawl onto agricultural land.

Cairo has some of the world's highest housing densities, with people living in cramped conditions at every level from ground to roof.

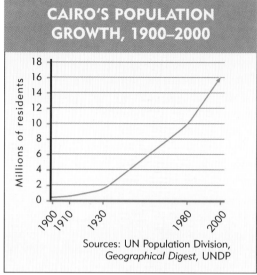

CAIRO'S POPULATION GROWTH, 1900–2000

Sources: UN Population Division, *Geographical Digest*, UNDP

OVERCROWDED HOUSING

About three million people are estimated to live in the 70-plus squatter settlements around the capital city. At least twice this number live in poor housing areas in old Cairo. Although buildings are structurally sounder than in most other cities in the developing world, there is nevertheless chronic overcrowding which leads to appalling living conditions. Cairo's poorest people are concentrated in two areas. One is the 'Cities of the Dead' (see page 33); the other is 'El-Zabbaleen', a community built around the city's main rubbish dump. Most of El-Zabbaleen's 25,000 inhabitants earn a living by sorting the waste into metals and plastics before selling it (see page 41).

INADEQUATE PUBLIC SERVICES

Homes in the old parts of Cairo and in poor neighbourhoods are not well connected to essential services such as safe drinking water, sewerage and electricity. Food, animal and industrial wastes are not safely disposed of. When wastes mingle with supplies of drinking water, diseases spread through lack of hygiene. Many people suffer from frequent stomach disorders and diarrhoea, and occasionally life-threatening outbreaks of typhoid and cholera occur.

AIR POLLUTION

The desert climate means that air pollution is worse in Cairo than in many other big cities. Lack of rain and low average wind speeds encourage the build-up of fumes in the lower atmosphere, and these get trapped between the lines of multi-storey buildings. But the basic cause of the air pollution is human – more than two million cars pass daily through city streets designed to take half a million at most. Stationary vehicles on congested roads constantly belch out toxic fumes, giving rise to a host of chronic respiratory illnesses. The Sphinx and other ancient monuments are being eaten away by acid pollution from urban traffic and industries.

URBAN SPRAWL

Cairo's growth has been rapid and largely unplanned. Thousands of hectares of high-quality agricultural land surrounding the city have already been built on and destroyed. The Great Pyramids at Giza (see page 46) were once separated from Cairo by desert,

Rubbish gathers unhygienically in parts of Cairo where no organised collection system exists.

The daily overload of traffic on Cairo's main streets is a major cause of harmful air pollution.

but now they have been engulfed by urban areas and are increasingly damaged by air pollution and leaking sewage.

The non-stop growth of Cairo's population is a major contributor to the city's declining conditions. A breathing space from this persistent growth is needed to deal with problems that already exist. But, with migrants continuing to flood into the capital in search of work, it seems that the situation is likely to worsen rather than improve.

CASE STUDY
CAIRO'S SEWAGE SYSTEM

Cairo's sewage system is one example of the difficulties faced by the city's authorities. The basic system dates from 1910, when just over half a million people were living in the capital. A major new system was installed in the early 1980s, with the help of overseas aid from the UK and the USA. But the city was growing so fast by then that laying the new sewers was restricted to certain parts of town. At that time Cairo's population was about ten million. Since then it has increased by at least 50 per cent and there has been no major upgrade to cope with the swell. The result is sewage on the streets, especially in poor areas of the city.

The closely-packed way in which people live in old Cairo makes it virtually impossible to add a modern system, even if the money for it was available. The narrow lanes and alleys, with cramped apartments and workshops mixed together, are unsuited to the construction work and pipe laying necessary to install a modern system of sanitation.

Cairo's metro system is clean and efficient.

PROBLEM SOLVING

In the attempt to improve standards of living in Cairo, one successful investment has been the construction of a metro system – the first in Africa. Another plan is an ambitious 20-year scheme to solve housing problems by building new settlements in the desert around the city.

HOUSING SOLUTIONS

According to the government, Egypt's housing problems can only be alleviated by building away from Cairo, because the city is too old and too overcrowded for new developments within the built-up area. There is a long-term plan for 44 new settlements to be finished by about 2020, together capable of housing some 15 million people. It is hoped that more than three million new jobs will be created at the same time.

To attract new residents, loans and mortgages for buying the new houses are being offered on favourable terms. Critics of the new towns plan say that it favours the middle classes, because the poor could not possibly afford the type of housing offered. They maintain that the government should not be spending vast sums on new settlements, when the three million or more poor people living in the old parts of Cairo are barely connected to essential services.

The first metro link along the east bank of the River Nile in Cairo was completed in 1989. The second (Line 2), which uses the first tunnel ever to be built under the Nile, links Giza (the site of the Pyramids) with Cairo University and the city centre. This was completed ahead of schedule in 2000. A third line, linking the city centre to the airport, is under consideration.

Travelling on Line 2 is easy compared with movement above ground. The train service is well organised, quick, comfortable and clean, and television screens entertain people waiting on the platforms. One particularly Islamic feature is that the first carriage on every train is for women only.

The metro saves more than two million daily commuters the nightmare of using the roads. Above ground, streets suffer gridlock every rush hour. Anything that reduces problems such as air pollution, traffic congestion and road accidents is to be welcomed.

PLANNED NEW SETTLEMENTS

* New cities
• Old/established cities

Sixth of October City is a new settlement raised out of the desert sands, about 40km from central Cairo. It is linked to the centre of Cairo by a newly built superhighway known as 26 July, with a journey time of about 20 minutes, traffic permitting.

Some housing here is for wealthy people. Closeness to Medialand theme park and a new 18-hole golf course are attractions for those who have money to spare. Overall, however, the new city's appearance is far from attractive, including large zones of identical multi-storey apartments. Many are little better than the slums of Cairo, being overcrowded and not particularly clean.

The roads in Sixth of October City do not suffer the appalling congestion of Cairo's busy streets.

A RESIDENT'S STORY

'I work in a hospital in the centre of Cairo. I am pleased that I moved to Sixth of October City with my wife and young family. In the capital, we could stand no longer all the pollution, crowds and noise.

'However, all is not as it should be here. There are few leisure facilities and the sense of community is lacking. We don't have many friends; all of our good friends still live in Cairo. Important services such as hospitals and nursery schools are not yet well developed. I blame the planners. The design of the houses is unimaginative with many tower blocks. It is not easy for people to meet and to mix because residential areas have been split up according to the price of the housing. Many people have come to escape poverty in rural Egypt and they are not used to town living. They are having difficulty finding work and do not have the money to maintain their houses properly. The residential district close to the industrial zone is an eyesore. It is deteriorating fast and already resembles some of the poorer parts of Cairo.'

Much of Sixth of October City is made up of unattractive modern tower blocks, surrounded in part by dirty and useless desert land.

ANCIENT ALEXANDRIA

Alexandria today, with about three-and-a-half million residents, is a fraction of Cairo's size. On the other hand, it is a much older city than Cairo and has had a glorious past. Planned by Alexander the Great in 331 BC, it was for 600 years the cultural capital of the ancient world. One of the Seven Wonders of the Ancient World – the Pharos (great lighthouse) – was

Fishing boats anchor in the harbour, overlooked by Fort Qaytbay on the site of the old Pharos.

built there on an island near the harbour. (Some remains of the Pharos have recently been found by underwater archaeologists.) After the Greco-Roman era, the city fell into decay and was only revived in the 1800s as a port after the French and British landed there.

CASE STUDY
THE LIBRARY OF ALEXANDRIA

Beneath its vast sloping roof, the new library has ten floors, including four basement levels.

The Ancient Library of Alexandria was founded by Ptolemy I in 288 BC. It housed copies of all known learning matter in the ancient world, and was a symbol of the city's immense cultural importance. Great intellectuals such as Euclid and Archimedes studied there. They had access to 700,000 volumes, but all were lost when the library burnt down in the third century AD.

The new Alexandria Library, *Bibliotecha Alexandrina*, has just been completed. The aim is to house and restore manuscripts and rare books from Egypt and the Arab world. An elegant glass and aluminium building has been constructed at a cost of US$170 million, of which about one-third came from donations. The library is doing much to restore Alexandria's international

reputation. It started with 400,000 books, but it will hold up to 8 million eventually.

The hope is that the library will help Alexandria to once again become a focus for overseas scholars from all parts of the Arab world, and that it will boost Egypt's status as the number one centre of learning in the region. Cairo is already an international city. If more scholars and visitors can be attracted to Alexandria, pressure on Cairo will be reduced. Some of the economic benefits of tourism will be spread and this will help to overcome the feeling that everything new and important must be built in Cairo. It is an attempt to restore the global profile of Alexandria, whose city rulers feel that it has floundered under the shadow of Egypt's current capital for too many years.

Egyptian holidaymakers flock to the beach and promenade along Alexandria's eastern harbour.

ALEXANDRIA'S FUNCTIONS

Alexandria's primary function remains as Egypt's main port and trading centre, through which 60 per cent of the country's imports pass. The commercial port has been deepened and enlarged in recent years to improve its capacity. Alexandria is also home to a wealth of small industries, mainly port-related.

The second function is as a tourist centre for Egyptians. Alexandria is very popular with people living in Cairo, mainly because of its beaches. What's more, the summer heat is not as sizzling here as it is in the capital. Visitors from Cairo notice two other big differences immediately. Air quality is better – sea breezes and clearer roads help. Secondly, traffic noise is less. In most Egyptian cities drivers use car horns rather than indicators – there is even a local saying that if the horn is broken, the car won't go! But in Alexandria, fines are imposed on drivers who use their horns excessively.

LOOKING AHEAD

Problems with housing, services and unemployment exist in Alexandria, but on a smaller scale than in Cairo. This makes them easier to solve. The population is growing, but not at such an alarming rate. Alexandria is now a much cleaner city than Cairo as well. This was not always the case, but recently private contractors from a French-owned waste management company have been employed to collect and handle waste from the beaches and urban areas. The scheme has been a great success, although only 40 per cent of the urban area is covered so far.

At the same time, the local government is improving and modernising the city's street furniture. More than 750,000 trees have been planted, many in poorer neighbourhoods, and Alexandria is now described as 'the best groomed city in Egypt'. The work of an enthusiastic city government is starting to make a difference. However, conservationists complain that Alexandria's valuable heritage is declining as historic villas are pulled down. Building speculators have erected hundreds of blocks of holiday flats along the coast for some 120km to the west of the town. The intention was to cater for influxes of Egyptian and other Arab holidaymakers, but many of the flats are still unfinished and unused.

Collecting waste for recyling helps to maintain the city's reputation as the cleanest in Egypt.

Tourist outlets, such as this T-shirt stall, support Egypt's local industries.

By world standards, Egypt is a poor country. Informal (unregistered) trade is rife and makes an important contribution to the economy. Exports such as oil, gas and cotton are also vital earners, though their relative value is low. 'Invisible' moneys from tourism, overseas workers and the Suez Canal are increasingly needed to boost the country's wealth.

Egypt is categorised as a less economically developed country (LEDC). One of the main measures used to show differences in wealth between countries is the GNI per capita (Gross National Income per head). In 2001 the GNI was US$1,530 per capita in Egypt. This was higher than in most other LEDCs, but much lower than in more economically developed countries (MEDCs) such as Germany (see graphs below).

GNI PER CAPITA (US$)

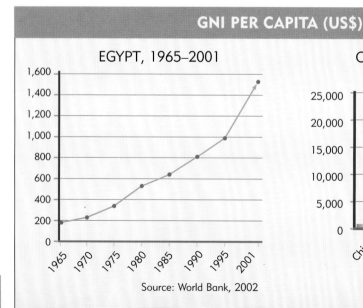

EGYPT, 1965–2001

Source: World Bank, 2002

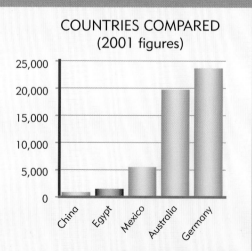

COUNTRIES COMPARED (2001 figures)

Source: World Bank, 2002

THE INFORMAL SECTOR

Egypt is a country of small businesses and businessmen, including shops, street hawkers and repairers of shoes, tyres, bikes and cars. About 80 per cent of these businesses operate outside the tax system and are not officially registered. This is the informal sector.

There are an estimated 6.5 million informal workers in Egypt. The old quarter of Cairo buzzes with a crazy mixture of repair shops, workshops and shops selling goods. Tourists are drawn to the great 'bazaar' area, where souvenir stalls line and almost fill the narrow streets. Businesses that would be run indoors

Hand-crafted souvenirs are sold all over Cairo.

in the UK are managed on the streets in Cairo, where an army of helpers, many very young, try to earn a living through petty services.

MANUFACTURING

Manufacturing employs 30 per cent of Egypt's registered workforce. Most of the industries are based on home needs – some are heavy industries such as oil refining, chemicals and concrete production, but the majority focus on making consumer goods. The largest of these industries is textiles (see page 55).

CASE STUDY
INFORMAL SECTOR IN EL-ZABBALEEN

Recycling litter is just one activity among the Zabbaleens, who provide a vital urban service.

El-Zabbaleen is a community of mostly Coptic Christians who make their living by collecting and recycling Cairo's rubbish. An estimated 75,000 are employed in the various connected businesses, worth about £7.5 million per year.

The system is well organised. It was founded about 100 years ago by a group known as the Wahiya. Today, descendants of the Wahiya collect rubbish from various Cairo districts and charge each household a monthly fee, equal to about 30 pence. They then pay the Zabbaleens to take the litter away. The Zabbaleens have varying jobs – some people are collectors, others are sorters, recyclers or dealers. It is dirty and unhealthy work, but they do a good service for Cairo's residents. What is more, they recycle 80 per cent of the rubbish – some councils in the UK recycle less than 10 per cent.

MAJOR TRADING PARTNERS (% GDP), 2001

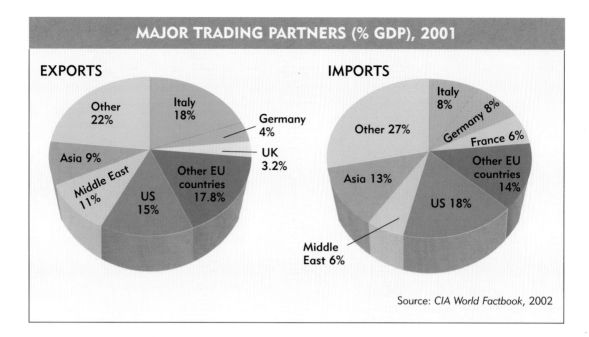

EXPORTS

- Other 22%
- Italy 18%
- Germany 4%
- UK 3.2%
- Other EU countries 17.8%
- US 15%
- Middle East 11%
- Asia 9%

IMPORTS

- Italy 8%
- Germany 8%
- France 6%
- Other EU countries 14%
- US 18%
- Middle East 6%
- Asia 13%
- Other 27%

Source: *CIA World Factbook*, 2002

FOREIGN TRADE

Egypt earns foreign exchange from both visible and invisible exports. Visible exports are goods sent overseas, which can be weighed or counted and given a value. Invisible exports are remittances (money) sent back home by Egyptians working abroad, as well as money earned from services rendered to international visitors or foreign companies.

Egypt's foreign trade is typical of many LEDCs in that it suffers from a large negative trade gap – as a country it spends more than twice as much on importing goods as it earns from exporting. Egypt's visible exports are mainly primary products. It does export some manufactured goods (such as fridges and other consumer durables, pharmaceutical products and garments) to countries in the Middle East and Africa – but quotas limit the amounts that Egypt can export to the USA and the EU, where the real money might be made.

The problem is, primary products tend to be lower in value than manufactured goods – and while Eygpt exports mainly the former, its imports are dominated by the latter. This creates the wide gap in value between imports and exports. Invisible earnings (see pages 44–45) are needed to try to close the gap.

VALUE OF VISIBLE IMPORTS AND EXPORTS, 2002

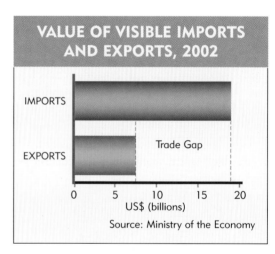

IMPORTS

EXPORTS

Trade Gap

0   5   10   15   20
US$ (billions)

Source: Ministry of the Economy

VISIBLE EXPORTS
OIL AND GAS

Another feature of trade in most LEDCs is an over-reliance on one type of export product – in Egypt's case, hydrocarbons (oil and natural gas). These are two of Egypt's major natural resources. The country's oil production peaked in 1995 at just below one million barrels per day; but by 2001, output had fallen to 640,000. Despite being an exporter, Egypt is not as rich in oil as countries such as Saudi Arabia. If its output continues to drop, Egypt will probably have to become an importer of oil instead.

This Red Sea oil well is just one of Egypt's many offshore fuel resources.

What is happening is that the economy is gradually changing its dependence from oil to natural gas. Large gas reserves exist in Egypt and, unlike oil, new reserves continue to be found. Previously most of the new discoveries were onshore – in the delta, the Western Desert and near the Gulf of Suez. Now they are mostly found offshore, in the shallow waters on the edge of the delta. Two large pipelines have been constructed to extract this gas for export in liquified form.

In some test drillings, gas has been found in every well sunk, which is very unusual in the oil and gas business. This suggests that great reserves of gas are still waiting to be found in the Mediterranean Sea. Gas companies are eager to drill into rocks below ever deeper waters further away from the coast. Nobody will be surprised if new gas finds eventually double the country's known reserves.

Egypt is fortunate that natural gas is now in great demand internationally. It is becoming a very popular fuel for generating electricity in Europe because it is cleaner than coal and oil. It produces lower carbon dioxide emissions, which means less global warming. Egypt has signed a long-term contract with power providers in Spain, guaranteeing a reliable income for the future. This has justified the enormous costs of building pipelines and extending the search into deeper waters.

AGRICULTURAL EXPORTS

There has been a decline in the export of agricultural goods from Egypt, because these are increasingly consumed by the country's expanding population. Cotton is the most important agricultural export. Egyptian cotton is known to be the best in the world – it is a strong variety that can be spun into the finest yarns. These are made into top-quality fabrics for international fashion markets.

Fruit and vegetables, such as oranges and potatoes, are also exported, mainly to Europe in winter – out-of-season demand is high and growing, which raises earnings and balances transport costs. Exports should increase if the new agricultural projects in the desert are a success (see pages 30–31). But the growth of cheap air freight allows US, European and Asian supermarkets to import fresh fruit and vegetables from all round the world, so Egypt's costs must be competitive if such exports are to expand significantly.

Egyptian cotton is the world's finest, but harvesting it is labour-intensive work.

INVISIBLE EXPORTS

TOURISM

By the year 2000, tourist revenues had grown to become Egypt's largest single earner of foreign income. Tourism is a useful economic activity and continues to grow in importance. The industry is explored in the next chapter.

EGYPTIANS WORKING OVERSEAS

Egypt's people are a vital resource. The country has a surplus of qualified engineers, teachers and other professionals who are much sought-after by other Arab countries and some other African nations. Education in schools, and particularly in universities, is longer established and of a higher standard than in neighbouring lands.

Countries around the Persian Gulf have much larger amounts of oil than Egypt, but smaller and less well-educated populations. Skilled workers from Egypt are in high demand in these places because they share the same religion and language. Cultural

Cairo University, where these students are gathered, is the largest and most prestigious centre of learning in the Arab-speaking world.

conflicts are less likely to arise with Egyptian employees than when non-Muslims from Western countries are recruited.

Egyptian people living in the Gulf countries tend to work long hours and spend as little money as possible. This means that much of what they earn can be sent back to their families in Egypt as remittances. Not only does this improve the standard of living of their families – it also benefits Egyptian workers and other branches of the Egyptian economy because the money is spent in their own country. On the negative side, however, it can cause significant personal problems with families often being split for years at a time.

SUEZ CANAL TARIFFS

The Suez Canal links the Mediterranean Sea with the Red Sea, providing a convenient route for ships from Europe to travel to and from the oilfields of the Middle East, India and the Far East. Every ship that passes through the Suez Canal is charged a fee based on its load. This earns about US$2 billion every year for the Egyptian economy. In 2000 more than 14,000 bulk carriers, oil and gas tankers, warships and passenger ships used the canal.

The Suez Canal cuts though desert landscape, providing a passage for ocean-going ships.

Cutting the 167km Suez Canal was an outstanding feat of nineteenth-century engineering. A channel almost 1km wide was built to link the chain of natural salt lakes (the Bitter Lakes) from the Mediterranean Sea in the north to the Gulf of Suez on the Red Sea in the south. It is the third-longest shipping canal in the world, after the South Lawrence Passage (USA) and the Maritime Channel at the Baltic Sea in Russia. No locks are needed – ships sail in convoy from each end and the Bitter Lakes are used as passing places.

The canal was opened in 1869 as a shortcut for ships travelling between Europe and Asia. It replaced the long route around the Cape of Good Hope at the southern tip of Africa. A Frenchman, Ferdinand de Lesseps, designed and supervised the canal's construction. It was a financial disaster for Egypt, which sold its shares in the canal to Britain in 1879. The canal was operated by the British until it was nationalised by President Nasser in 1953.

Since nationalisation, the Suez Canal has been improved several times by digging by-pass channels. It can now accommodate the largest ships, as long as they are not fully laden. Oil tankers can offload part of their cargo at the south end of the canal, and this is pumped through a pipeline to Alexandria where it can be reloaded. Most tonnage travels from the resource-rich countries south of the canal to the more industrialised countries north of it. The canal can handle 80 ships a day, but on average only about 40 are passing through. This still represents some 6 per cent of the world's sea-borne trade.

The challenge for Egypt is to increase the use of the canal and its income. At present, a US$400 million project is underway to deepen the channel to 20m – but if it is to attract a higher proportion of oil movements between the Middle East and Europe, it needs to be deeper still. Within the next 10 years, the hope is that it can be dredged to more than 30m in depth, which would allow almost all of the world's largest oil tankers to pass through when fully laden. This would give a huge boost to revenues, because at the moment these vast tankers still travel around the Cape of Good Hope when fully loaded.

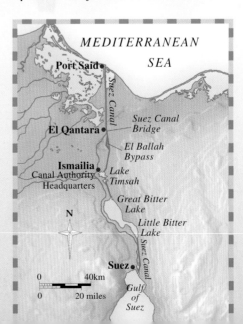

TOURISM

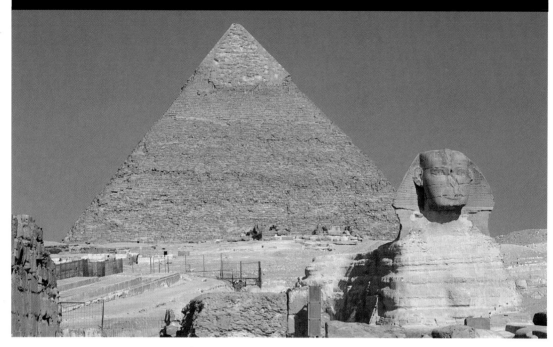

The Sphinx and the Great Pyramids are world-renowned visitor attractions.

Tourism is a long-established industry in Egypt – among the amazing pyramids, temples, palaces and statues there is a richer collection of antiquities than in any other country. Luxor lies at the centre of the zone of ancient sites, and a new tourist area has grown up next to the Red Sea, where sun and sea are the attractions. Tourism brings many economic advantages, but it also leaves some problems in its wake.

A HISTORIC INDUSTRY

Egypt was the birthplace of the package tour holiday. In the second half of the nineteenth century, English entrepreneur Thomas Cook took wealthy Victorians on organised visits to Cairo and the Nile valley as part of a 'Grand Tour'. By 1900, tourism in Egypt was already booming, with grand hotels established in Cairo (Shepheard's), Luxor (the Winter Palace) and Aswan (the Cataract). These and luxury Nile boats enabled European royalty and aristocrats to visit the spectacular ancient sites in supreme comfort and style.

Tourism is still big business in Egypt. Three regions are important – in and around Cairo, Upper Egypt from Luxor southwards, and next to the Red Sea. In the first two, tourism dates back to Cook's time, but the Red Sea is a new

destination. It differs from the others in that its main attractions are natural rather than cultural. In all of these areas, an army of people – including camel drivers, guides and hawkers – make a living from selling services to tourists. They are part of the large informal sector that tourism supports.

IN AND AROUND CAIRO

For many people, Cairo's most exciting sights lie just outside the city. The Great Pyramids and the Sphinx are located in the suburb of Giza, 11km south-west of the centre. The site is dominated by three pyramids – the most vast and best preserved of the 80-plus pyramids built in the northern Nile valley. The largest is the Great Pyramid of Cheops, which measures a monumental 137m high.

Close to the Great Pyramids is the Sphinx, a symbolic statue that stands an impressive 20m high. It was sculpted from a solid limestone block and has the body of a lion and the head of a god or god-like man.

Within the city, the foremost museum is the Egyptian Antiquities Museum. Its two greatest attractions are treasures from the tomb of Tutankhamun, and the mummies of Ramses II and other pharaohs. Medieval Cairo is the most visited part of the city. Outside the walls of the Citadel (a complex of massive stone fortifications) is the densest collection of mosques in Egypt. The one that stands out is El-Azhar Mosque (see below).

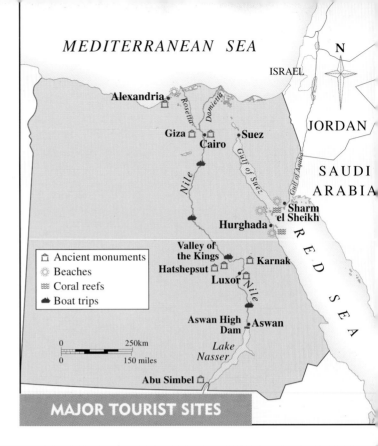

MAJOR TOURIST SITES

CASE STUDY
EL-AZHAR MOSQUE

In a scene that has changed little for more than a thousand years, students of Islam can regularly be found in the El-Azhar Mosque, sitting cross-legged on the floor beneath the pillars of the central court. Grouped around their tutors, they study the Koran in the time-honoured manner.

This great building, completed in AD 971, is both a mosque and a university. Its 20,000 or more students are drawn not just from Egypt, but also from all Muslim countries within and beyond the Arab world. Although the cities of Mecca and Medina in Saudi Arabia are better known to non-Muslims as Islam's holy centres, El-Azhar is the leading place of learning for Sunni Muslims and is respected throughout the Islamic world. This is why students and teachers come here from Muslim nations as far away as Indonesia and Malaysia in the east and Morocco in the west. Like other monuments, the mosque provides

The El-Azhar Mosque is famous throughout the Muslim world. It supports the Egyptian economy by attracting international visitors and students.

a source of 'invisible income' for Egypt by attracting international interest. It is located amid the city's greatest concentration of holy buildings and visitor attractions.

ABOVE: The Temple of Luxor, located alongside the Nile, is an important ancient landmark.
RIGHT: Boats of many different shapes and sizes are used to take tourists up and down the Nile.

VISITING UPPER EGYPT

Luxor is only a small town, but it is the centre for the most fascinating collection of ancient remains in Egypt. In and around the town are enormous temples, giant statues and unique tombs. Almost everyone makes a living out of tourism. The international airport is used by charter airlines from Europe, so visitors can bypass the congestion and concrete of Cairo.

Dominating the town centre on the east bank of the Nile is the Temple of Luxor, with two grand statues of Ramses II at its entrance. An avenue lined with small sphinxes leads into the Temple of Karnak, 5km to the north. The size and scale of Karnak is awesome. As it was the spiritual centre of the ancient kingdom, it was continually added to over a period of 1,300 years. Within it is the Great Temple of Amun, one of the most revered Egyptian gods.

On the west bank, towards the Valleys of the Kings and Queens, are temples built against a stunning background of arid mountains. In the Valley of the Kings more than 100 tombs, where the pharaohs were buried with their treasures, are tunnelled deep into the hill-sides. Of these, the tomb of Tutankhamun was the only one that had escaped looters and remained intact when archaeologists discovered it in modern times.

AROUND ASWAN

Nile cruises to Aswan begin in Luxor. It is a scenic boat ride. The strip of cultivated land narrows and the desert walls of the valley close in towards Aswan. Although many people visit the High Dam, and may even sail on Lake Nasser, the highlight of any visit to Upper Egypt is the Great Temple of Ramses II at Abu Simbel (see case study opposite).

RED SEA RESORTS

In recent years, an increasing number of coastal resorts have been springing up around the beaches of the Red Sea. An airport has opened up at the expanding settlement of Sharm el Sheikh, near the southern tip of the Sinai peninsula, and this has caused dramatic growth in the local tourist industry. Likewise, the construction of numerous four-and five-star bayside hotels has acted as a magnet for holidaymakers, particularly those arriving on

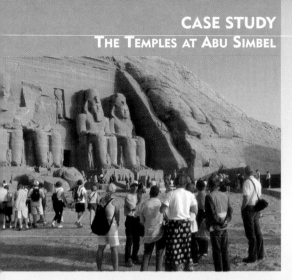

The appeal of Abu Simbel is powerful enough to draw visitors to the remote south of Egypt.

Ramses II built two twin temples at Abu Simbel – one for himself and the other for his wife Nefertari. Four gigantic, seated figures of the king guard the main entrance, making up one of Egypt's most stunning sights. Thousands of visitors flock to see them and they contribute significantly to Egypt's tourist trade. However, the temples are not seen today in their original location.

When the Aswan High Dam was proposed, the planned floodplain for Lake Nasser threatened to swamp the massive buildings and destroy an important part of the country's cultural heritage. Realising the damage that this would also do to the national economy, the Egyptian government secured funding from UNESCO to remove and reconstruct the temples away from danger. In a project that took US$40 million and two years to complete (1966–1968) the temples were hand-sawn into more than 1,000 pieces, carved from the cliff in which they sat and reassembled block-by-block on an artificial hill, some 61m higher up and more than 200m further west. The cliff was also recreated at the new site, so that the temples could be admired in their proper context. Lake Nasser was too important for the Egyptians not to be built, but the temples were too important to the world and to Egyptian tourism to be drowned by lake water.

package tours from Europe. Wealthy people from Cairo, too, are drawn to the Red Sea to get away from the hustle of the city. Gently shelving beaches make these resorts ideal for families, and guaranteed year-round sunshine with warm winter temperatures are a bonus.

There are very few tourist sites that are accessible inland from the Red Sea resorts. What most attracts visitors are the coral reefs that lie offshore. The Red Sea reefs are superb – a scuba diver's and snorkeller's paradise. The reefs just to the north of Sharm el Sheikh are particularly stunning with their bright coral shelves teeming with shoals of colourful fish, white tipped-sharks and rays (see also page 57).

Most visitors seem unperturbed by the fact that the outskirts of the Red Sea resorts often resemble construction sites, and that many of the beaches are made of dusty, reddish grit instead of sand. As the resorts expand, it is likely that some of them will merge together to form continuous built-up strips.

At Sharm el Sheikh, the beach is the focus. Boats take divers and snorkellers out to the reefs.

TOURIST REVENUE

The economic advantages of tourism to Egypt are great. Nearly 150,000 registered workers are directly employed by this trade, and added to these are many more in the informal sector. Tourism is a vital source of foreign exchange. In the peak year of 2000/01, tourist receipts approached US$5 billion for the first time – the spendings of more than 400,000 visitors.

Tourism often provides jobs in places where other employment opportunities are limited or non-existent. Luxor is a fine example of a place where tourism is the only economic activity. The industry provides work of many types – in the hotels, on the Nile boats and at the monuments. It is also generating economic development along the Red Sea coast, a region that hitherto suffered because of its remoteness from population centres in the Nile valley. This has led to a massive boom in construction work – 80 per cent of the new hotel rooms being built in Egypt in 2001 were located in the Red Sea and South Sinai areas.

Expansion of tourism is one of the few options for economic growth that exist for many less economically developed countries. Tourists are a means for money to be transferred from rich countries to poor.

The carving of alabaster souvenirs is just one of the many craft industries that tourism supports.

Guaranteed sun and year-round heat are natural resources that Egyptians take for granted, but they are in scarce supply in northern Europe and Russia for much of the year. It is mainly for visitors from these two areas that the Red Sea resorts are being so rapidly expanded. This is coastal tourism, a type that is common around much of the Mediterranean, but relatively new to Egypt. Diversification like this into different branches of tourism helps to reduce peaks and troughs in visitor numbers throughout the seasons.

ECONOMIC PROBLEMS

Unfortunately, numbers of tourists can vary wildly from year to year, and this has an impact on the economy. Egypt has suffered several severe blows to the tourist industry (see case study opposite) which have forced the country to channel considerable resources into restoring the damage. However, Egypt's powers of recovery have been impressive. There is no shortage of people wanting to take cultural and coastal holidays in Egypt, provided they feel it is safe to go there.

In October 1997, 58 foreigners and four Egyptians were massacred in Luxor by Islamic militants. This made international headlines and Egypt was hit hard. For at least 12 months afterwards, Luxor's 70,000 inhabitants could do no more than look at the rows of empty horse-drawn carriages and masses of lifeless cruise boats along the banks of the Nile. January to March 1998 should have been the high season, with all accommodation taken – but most hotels barely reached 20 per cent occupancy, and monuments were empty of visitors. A survey showed that up to half of the local tour operators had to lay off staff. Others reduced wages by 50 per cent. Without tourism, everyone in Luxor suffered because there was no alternative industry.

This was a home-based problem; Egypt was, therefore, able to search for its own solutions. Security was tightened up strongly, with the obvious presence of both armed and plain-clothed police at the historical sites, in the hotels and on the roads. The Tourism Ministry ran a global public relations and information campaign to lure back frightened visitors. Big discounts were offered and tourists began to drift back. Finally, visitor numbers peaked at record levels in the 2000/1 season.

The next big blow happened outside Egypt. After the terrorist attacks in New York on 11 September 2001, global tourism took a dramatic downturn. A US$2 billion shortfall in Egypt's earnings resulted and thousands of workers in the hotel sector were laid off.

Many of Luxor's hotels are designed for wealthy tourists, whose revenue is vital to the economy.

However, with the help of discounted prices, by the end of 2002 tourist numbers had reached 98 per cent of previous levels.

Tourism hit another slump in 2003. This time it was due to fears about turmoil in the Middle East and the war in Iraq – events that again were out of Egypt's control. Once more, Egypt fought back to restore international faith.

Horse-drawn carriages provide a relaxing way for visitors to enjoy the sights of Luxor.

SOCIAL, ECONOMIC AND ENVIRONMENTAL ISSUES

Many of Egypt's educated young people lack the chance to use their skills.

The government of Egypt faces many problematic issues. These include social concerns resulting from the spread of extreme religious groups, financial troubles due mainly to the weakness of the economy and the need for it to grow, and some serious environmental issues that are increasingly being highlighted by conservationists.

RELIGIOUS EXTREMES

Some Muslims try to impose on everyone a strict, or extreme, version of the laws set out in the Koran. They are known as Islamic fundamentalists. Support for fundamentalism is increasing throughout the Islamic world, including Egypt – but Egypt is different from some of the other Islamic states because it has a constitution that guarantees freedom of religion. Also, there is a significant Coptic Christian minority who campaign to be fairly represented. The government has moved to address some of the Copts' grievances in the past few years. State radio and television channels carry live broadcasts of Christmas and Easter masses, both of them Christian festivals that are not celebrated by Muslims.

During the late 1990s, the extreme Islamic group *Gama'a al-Islamiya* was responsible for a catalogue of incidents involving foreign tourists. In April 1996, its gunmen shot dead 18 Greek tourists at their hotel near the Giza pyramids, apparently mistaking them for Israelis. In September 1997, two brothers burnt and shot dead nine German tourists and their Egyptian driver outside the Egyptian Museum in the centre of Cairo. The October 1997 Luxor killings (see page 51) were carried out by the same fundamentalist group.

At first the government was reluctant to acknowledge that a problem existed – but, due to its disastrous economic consequences, the Luxor incident changed things. Since then, there has been a crack-down on the activities of *Gama'a* and increased surveillance of other extremist groups, most notably Islamic *Jihad* and the Muslim Brotherhood. This proactive government policy is popular with the vast majority of Egyptians, who resent the actions of the violent fundamentalist minority.

ECONOMIC ISSUES

The standard of living for the average Egyptian is improving, but only slowly. In the first years of the new millennium, Egypt's population has continued to escalate and the country still faces difficult times. The economy is not growing fast enough to:

- create new jobs and employ all school and university leavers
- significantly improve the standard of living of most Egyptians and relieve poverty
- balance the financial books in overseas trade by increasing export earnings.

GEOGRAPHICAL PROBLEMS

One reason for Egypt's slow economic growth was beyond the control of its government – the country's proximity to the Middle East, a region of continuing political instability. Although not directly involved in the struggle between Israelis and Palestinians, or the war in Iraq, Egypt's closeness to the areas of conflict made overseas companies less willing to invest and tourists less willing to visit. Egypt's two other sources of foreign currency – earnings from ships on the Suez Canal and remittances from workers overseas – also fell, as uncertainty over the situation in Iraq and the Middle East caused a slump in the world economy during 2003.

UNEMPLOYMENT

A stagnant economy could not have come at a worse time for the Egyptian government. It needed 900,000 new jobs a year just to stop the unemployment rate from rising. According to the government the official unemployment rate was 9 per cent, but independent estimates put it much higher, at between 11 and 20 per cent. Most worrying of all was the fact that 15–30-year-olds were the ones most likely to be out of work. These are the people upon whom the future growth of Egypt depends. They are the ones who will really determine Egypt's direction and prosperity in the twenty-first century. At the moment many young people are forced to scratch out a living in the informal sector, where the availability of work is erratic and low paid where it exists. In many cases, they have skills and education that go to waste due to lack of opportunity in the job market.

TELECOMMUNICATIONS DATA	
Mainline Phones (1998)	3,971,500
Moblie Phones (1999)	380,000
Internet Service Providers (2001)	50

Source: *CIA World Factbook*, 2002

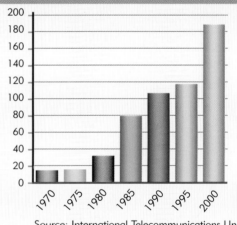

TELEVISION SETS PER 1,000 PEOPLE

Source: International Telecommunications Union

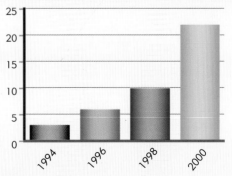

PERSONAL COMPUTERS PER 1,000 PEOPLE

Source: World Development Indicators, World Bank

Large Projects

Throughout history, Egyptians have famously undertaken large projects, as demonstrated by the pyramids and temples, the Suez Canal and the Aswan High Dam. The government's present 'mega project' is the South Valley Development Project (see pages 30–31). It is hoped that this will successfully encourage millions of Egyptians to move to the desert, away from the overcrowded Nile valley.

The advantages of the South Valley scheme could be great, including greater crop yields, more agricultural exports and reduced urban crowding. Critics, however, question whether all the possible advantages will actually be realised when the project is up and running. Will some of its potential go to waste? The Egyptians have been turning strips of desert green for centuries, but what is different about this scheme is that it is taking place far away from the Nile valley. No one has traditionally lived a settled life this deep in the desert. Will people be willing to move there and work? Will the infrastructure of any new settlement be strong enough to sustain long-term development? Familiar farming problems such as salination may be partly anticipated – but will there be unforeseen difficulties such as shifting sands?

The Temple at Hatshepsut (near Luxor) is spectacular both for its size and setting. Dating from 1450 BC, it was one of the earliest large projects to be embarked on in ancient Egypt.

Some people fear that the scheme might prove to be a 'white elephant', draining government funds that could have been used to stimulate other sectors of the economy. Could the massive sums of money being spent have been spent better elsewhere? Others reply that critics said the same when the Aswan High Dam was first proposed, and that this project has since proved its worth.

Manufacturing Concerns

Some developing countries in other parts of the world have enjoyed great economic growth since 1960. The key factor responsible for this was a big expansion in manufacturing. The 'Asian Tigers' (Hong Kong, Singapore, South Korea and Taiwan) were examples, as were Brazil and Mexico in the Americas. Multinational companies invested heavily in these countries to take advantage of their cheaper labour and lower costs of production. Factories were built so that the goods made could be sold worldwide, in the global market. Why has this not happened in Egypt? After all, it is closer to the EU and its wealthy consumers than the countries named above.

There has been some foreign investment into Egypt. The Mercedes car factory (see below) is one example, although it is only a small-scale operation. However, foreign investment makes up less than 2 per cent of Egypt's GDP. Overseas companies have been put off by the pile of regulations designed to help Egypt's local producers, and by the bureaucracy (lengthy processing of paperwork) that the Egyptian government imposes.

The trouble with protecting home industries is that it does not encourage efficiency. The state-run textile industries in Egypt employ huge numbers – about one-quarter of the manufacturing workforce. In one sense it is good that so much employment exists. The problem is that these industries operate

Egypt's textile industry employs more people than any other manufacturing sector. It benefits from fine cotton, but lack of modern equipment means that many items are poorly made.

at a loss. They lack modern machinery, their goods are often of poor quality, and managers do not have the marketing skills to make them more competitive internationally.

CASE STUDY
MERCEDES CAR FACTORY, SIXTH OF OCTOBER CITY

Unusually for Egypt, the assembly line in the Mercedes car factory is highly mechanised.

A Mercedes factory was set up in Sixth of October City in 1996, and it makes every one of the 1,600 Mercedes cars sold in Egypt every year. The company said that it came to Egypt for two reasons. Firstly, Egypt has the largest market for cars in the region – about 70,000 per year. Secondly, the country's duties (taxes) on imported cars are a crippling 230 per cent, making it impractical to buy cars from abroad.

Despite all the rules and regulations, the Mercedes car plant is profitable. Low operating costs explain this. Wages for the 400 workers are one-fifth of those paid to workers in the company's German plants, even though the Egyptians work to similar standards. Another incentive was tax-free income for 10 years, offered by the government to potential industries as part of the new towns plan.

If Mercedes wants to export vehicles from Egypt, there is a problem. Tax rules make it virtually impossible to export cars out of Egypt. Company managers think that one way around the regulations might be to export car parts to the company's factories in other countries. By making parts for the global market, it should be possible to achieve 'economies of scale' (greater quantities leading to lower production costs).

CONSERVATION ISSUES

The government of Egypt has come under increased pressure from conservation groups to consider environmental issues more seriously than it has done in the past. There has often been a significant gap between political rhetoric (what the government says) and practice (what the government does).

Environmental problems are abundant in Egypt. They are most acute in and around Cairo – mainly a reflection of the city's size. Atmospheric pollution, water pollution from chemical works on the banks of the Nile, problems with disposal of food, animal and industrial waste from inside Cairo, and the sprawl of new towns outside it, are just four of the serious environmental issues. Cleaning up urban areas is going to be a huge task.

One of the few hopeful signs is the country's switch to gas. Natural gas is the cleanest and most environmentally acceptable of the fossil fuels. Its use as the fuel for generating electricity and powering road vehicles has begun and looks set to grow significantly. The big hope for the citizens of Cairo in their quest for clean air is CNG (Compressed Natural Gas). This releases 85 per cent fewer exhaust emissions than petrol and diesel and is increasingly available in garages.

ABOVE: The Sphinx and other monuments are being worn away by serious air pollution and vandalism due to Cairo's continuing expansion. MAIN PICTURE: Chemical plants, such as this one near Alexandria, emit damaging toxic fumes.

CASE STUDY
DAMAGE TO THE RED SEA REEFS

The coral reef is an attractive but fragile ecoystem, easily damaged by tourism.

Coral reefs are colonies of tiny marine creatures that make up a colourful shelf off certain stretches of coast. In the clear waters of the Red Sea, they are a beautiful sight, alive with fish and a delight for divers. However, every time a diving boat drops anchor, the reef is damaged and the coral can die. With more than 700 boats operating from the Red Sea resort of Hurghada alone, the potential for damage is huge. Most boats make two trips a day provided there is the demand, though they don't all run at the same time.

HEPCA (Hurghada Environmental Protection Conservation Association) was formed in 1992. It operates a training programme for local boat owners and has placed mooring buoys for boats at the most popular diving sites. The reefs are patrolled by national park rangers. Gradually, the rules against dropping anchors on the reefs are being enforced more strictly.

TOURISM AND THE ENVIRONMENT

The Red Sea region suffers the most severe environmental problems arising from tourism. Building hotel resorts along the shores of the Red Sea went ahead with such speed that no one gave a thought to possible consequences for the environment. The key problems were excessive coastal development and poor waste disposal. Visitors began to descend on the area without any control on numbers or on activities undertaken. Environmentalists felt that there was a real risk of destruction of the natural attractions that the visitors had come to see, particularly the coral reefs.

Today, anyone who proposes a new hotel development is obliged to carry out an environmental impact assessment and present it to the Egyptian Environmental Affairs Authority. Under persistent pressure from environmental organisations, officials are now making more rigorous checks. About one-third of the schemes are turned down, which suggests that the new system, while not perfect, involves more than just casual rubber-stamping. An official from the Tourism Ministry has talked about the need for 'sustainable tourism' along the coast, and this is seen as a hopeful sign that people are looking ahead with long-term goals.

EGYPT'S FUTURE

Egypt has some superb natural attractions, and a cultural heritage that no other country can match. The last thing that anyone wants is any further damage and destruction to the nation's natural and historical treasures. The challenge that politicians, religious leaders, businessmen and environmental organisations face is finding a way to capitalise on these assets without destroying them. They need to balance the demands of an expanding tourist market with the basic needs of their growing population. The struggle for Egypt is in achieving a harmony that allows all of its inhabitants to enjoy a consistently acceptable standard of living. With its young, dynamic workforce and a wealth of natural resources, it has the potential to succeed.

GLOSSARY

Arid A term used to describe an environment that receives an annual rainfall of below 250–300mm.

Barchan A crescent-shaped sand dune, common in deserts such as the Sahara.

Bedouins Nomadic tribes of desert dwellers who move around with herds of camels and goats.

Birth rate The number of children born in a year per 1,000 population.

Constitution The agreed basic principles of a national government, controlling how it operates.

Coral reef An offshore ridge, built up over thousands of years, made of calcareous (limestone) substances from millions of small marine creatures.

Delta A triangular area of flat land near the mouth of some rivers, where sediment is deposited as the river meets the sea.

Density The number of people or other items per unit area.

Distributaries The branches of a river that flow away from the main stream in a delta.

Diversification Broadening an economy or business by adding new activities.

Economic To do with money, producing an income or earning a living.

Emissions Waste gases and solids released into the atmosphere by factories and vehicle exhausts.

Erosion The wearing away of soil or rock by the forces of nature or the actions of people.

EU (European Union) The group of countries in Europe that have united to achieve closer political, social, economic and environmental cooperation.

Floodplain Flat land on the banks of a river, made of silt soils that are deposited during flooding.

Foreign exchange Money from other countries, such as US dollars and the Euro, which can be used to pay for goods bought from other countries.

Fundamentalist A person who wants rules, laws, traditions or practices from earlier times to be followed rigidly today.

GDP (Gross Domestic Product) The total monetary value of goods and services produced by a country in a single year.

GNI (Gross National Income) Sometimes called the Gross National Product, or GNP, this is the total value of goods and services produced by a country, plus any earnings from overseas, in a single year.

Hydrocarbon Compounds of hydrogen and carbon, including oil and natural gas.

Hydroelectric power (HEP) Electricity generated by the force of water as it passes through turbines.

Informal sector Small businesses or people working in a self-help manner, without being registered with the authorities.

Invisible export Money earned by selling services rather than goods, for example tourist revenue and money sent back by citizens working overseas.

Irrigation The controlled addition of water to land to improve plant growth.

Islam One of the major world religions, based upon the teachings of the Prophet Mohammed and his laws written down in the Koran.

Khamsin A very hot, dry and dusty wind that blows from the Sahara Desert.

Koran The sacred book for Muslims – a collection of Mohammed's teachings, written in Arabic.

Less Economically Developed Country (LEDC) One of the world's less wealthy countries that are not part of the so-called 'Western' world.

Life expectancy The expected lifetime of a person born in any particular year – measured in years.

Meander A loop-like bend in a river.

Mega city A very large urban area with more than 10 million inhabitants.

Migration The movement of people, either temporary or permanent, from place to place.

Minaret A narrow tower at the top of a mosque, from which the regular call to prayer is issued.

Mortality rate (or death rate) The number of people who die in a year per 1,000 population.

Mosque A place of worship for Muslims – the equivalent of a church for Christians.

Multi-purpose scheme A large-scale project, such as the building of a dam, that will have many uses.

Muslim A follower of the religion Islam.

Natural increase The excess of births over deaths.

Nile Basin Initiative (NBI) A scheme involving ten countries from the Nile valley who are co-operating to manage water supplies from the River Nile.

Oasis An area of water within a desert. Water is likely to make the immediate area green, in contrast to the bare land surrounding it.

Petty services Services that provide for the everyday needs of people.

Quota A form of control or rationing that states a limit, for example the amount of goods that one country can export to another.

Ramadan The holy month of the Islamic year, during which Muslims do not eat, drink or smoke between sunrise and sunset.

Reclamation (of land) Changing infertile land into land that can be used for cultivation.

Remittances Sums of money sent to a person or sent back to a country from citizens who are working overseas.

Salination An unhealthy build-up of natural salts in the surface of the soil. Salination occurs with large-scale irrigation and can render land infertile.

Silt Fine-grained sediment deposited by rivers. Silt makes a good soil for farming because it is rich, fertile and easy to work.

Trade gap The difference in value between exports and imports. Egypt has a negative trade gap – the cost of its imports exceeds the value of its exports.

Trade winds Regular winds that blow from the north-east in the northern hemisphere.

Tributary A stream or river that flows into the main channel of a river.

Visible exports Goods sent to other countries, earning money for the country that produced them.

Wadi A steep-sided, gorge-like valley in a desert, without any river flowing in it for most of the time.

Wilderness A place where the forces of nature dominate, without any changes made by people.

FURTHER INFORMATION

BOOKS TO READ:

For geographical information, travel guides are useful. Look for recent editions. Examples are:

Eyewitness Travel Guides: Egypt (Dorling Kindersley, 2001)

Globetrotter Travel Guide: Egypt by Robin Gauldie (New Holland Publishers, 2004)

Lonely Planet: Egypt by Andrew Humphreys, Siona Jenkins (Lonely Planet, 2002)

The Rough Guide to Egypt by Dan Richardson (Rough Guides, 2003)

For information of a more historical nature, try:

The British Museum Book of Ancient Egypt by Stephen Quirke (British Museum, 1996)

Eyewitness Guide: Ancient Egypt by George Hart (Dorling Kindersley, 2002)

Horrible Histories: The Awesome Egyptians by Terry Deary (Scholastic, 1993)

Visiting the Past: The Pyramids by Jane Shuter (Heinemann Library, 2003)

For a scientific account of how the pyramids were built, try this book by a mechanical engineer:

The Giza Power Plant: Technologies of Ancient Egypt by Christoper Dunn (Bear and Company, 1998)

WEBSITES:

www.sis.gov.eg The official site of the Egypt State Information Service. This is a live site with current information on all aspects of life in Egypt. Headings are clear and all in English.

www.ancientegypt.co.uk The British Museum site. Headings range from Geography to Mummification and there are chances for interactive exploration.

www.guardians.net The site of Egypt's Supreme Council of Antiquities. This is described as the 'One-stop Gateway to Ancient Egypt'.

www.touregypt.net The official website for the Egyptian Ministry of Tourism. Within the tourist information are plenty of geographical details.

www.cia.gov/cia/publications/factbook/geos/eg.html The *CIA World Factbook* provides a wealth of up-to-date information and statistics on all aspects of life in Egypt and other countries.

www.egypttoday.com An online magazine that offers up-to-date news and tourist information.

USEFUL ADDRESS:

The Egyptian Embassy
26 South Street
London W1Y 6DD

INDEX

Numbers shown in **bold** refer to pages with maps, graphic illustrations or photographs.

Camel-riding in the barren Eastern Desert.

A Nile valley farmer and his donkey.